Timeless Seeds of Advice

The Sayings of the Prophet

(Peace be upon him)

In the English Language and Arabic

The Sayings of the Prophet

Copyright

King Fahd Complex for Printing

Editor/Writer: Noah Ibn Kathir, Imam Ahamd

All rights reserved. No part of this book may be reproduced or transmitted in any form or by any means, electronic or mechanical, including photocopying, recording, or by any information storage and retrieval system, without written permission from the Publisher.

The Sayings of the Prophet

O mankind, indeed We have created you from male and female and made you peoples and tribes that you may know one another. Indeed, the most noble of you in the sight of Allah is the most righteous of you. Indeed, Allah is Knowing and Acquainted. [49:13]

يَٰٓأَيُّهَا ٱلنَّاسُ إِنَّا خَلَقْنَٰكُم مِّن ذَكَرٍ وَأُنثَىٰ وَجَعَلْنَٰكُمْ شُعُوبًا وَقَبَآئِلَ لِتَعَارَفُوٓا۟ۚ إِنَّ أَكْرَمَكُمْ عِندَ ٱللَّهِ أَتْقَىٰكُمْۚ إِنَّ ٱللَّهَ عَلِيمٌ خَبِيرٌ ﴿١٣﴾

The Sayings of the Prophet

The Sayings of the Prophet

Preface

Indeed, all praise is due to Allāh, Lord of the worlds. We praise Him, seek refuge with Him, and seek His Forgiveness. We seek refuge with Allāh from the evils of our souls (nafs), and the mistakes in our actions. Whoever Allāh Guides, there is none who can misguide him, and whoever Allāh misguides, there is none who can guide him. And I testify that there is none worthy of being worshipped except Allāh, and I testify that Prophet Muhammad, peace and blessings be upon him, is his servant and Last Messenger.

O you who have believed, fear Allah as He should be feared and do not die except as Muslims [in submission to Him]. [3:102]

يَٰٓأَيُّهَا ٱلَّذِينَ ءَامَنُوا۟ ٱتَّقُوا۟ ٱللَّهَ حَقَّ تُقَاتِهِۦ وَلَا تَمُوتُنَّ إِلَّا وَأَنتُم مُّسْلِمُونَ ۝

The Sayings of the Prophet

O mankind, fear your Lord, who created you from one soul and created from it its mate and dispersed from both of them many men and women. And fear Allah, through whom you ask one another, and the wombs. Indeed Allah is ever, over you, an Observer. [4:1]

يَـٰٓأَيُّهَا ٱلنَّاسُ ٱتَّقُوا۟ رَبَّكُمُ ٱلَّذِى خَلَقَكُم مِّن نَّفْسٍ وَٰحِدَةٍ وَخَلَقَ مِنْهَا زَوْجَهَا وَبَثَّ مِنْهُمَا رِجَالًا كَثِيرًا وَنِسَآءً ۚ وَٱتَّقُوا۟ ٱللَّهَ ٱلَّذِى تَسَآءَلُونَ بِهِۦ وَٱلْأَرْحَامَ ۚ إِنَّ ٱللَّهَ كَانَ عَلَيْكُمْ رَقِيبًا ۝١

O you who have believed, fear Allah and speak words of appropriate justice. [33:70]

يَـٰٓأَيُّهَا ٱلَّذِينَ ءَامَنُوا۟ ٱتَّقُوا۟ ٱللَّهَ وَقُولُوا۟ قَوْلًا سَدِيدًا ۝٧٠

He will [then] amend for you your deeds and forgive you your sins. And whoever obeys Allah and His Messenger has certainly attained a great attainment. [33:71]

يُصْلِحْ لَكُمْ أَعْمَـٰلَكُمْ وَيَغْفِرْ لَكُمْ ذُنُوبَكُمْ ۗ وَمَن يُطِعِ ٱللَّهَ وَرَسُولَهُۥ فَقَدْ فَازَ فَوْزًا عَظِيمًا ۝٧١

The Sayings of the Prophet

Indeed, the most truthful of speech is the Speech of Allāh, and the best guidance is the guidance of Prophet Muhammad, peace and blessings be upon him. The worst of affairs are those that are newly introduced, and every newly introduced affair is an innovation, and every innovation is a misguidance, and every misguidance leads to the Fire. Kind speech and forgiveness are better than charity followed by injury. And Allah is Free of need and Forbearing. [2:263]

﴿ قَوْلٌ مَّعْرُوفٌ وَمَغْفِرَةٌ خَيْرٌ مِّن صَدَقَةٍ يَتْبَعُهَآ أَذًى ۗ وَاللَّهُ غَنِيٌّ حَلِيمٌ ﴾ ﴿٢٦٣﴾

As for what follows: Allāh sent Prophet Muhammad, peace and blessings be upon him, with the pure, easy religion and the comprehensive, inclusive Sharī'ah that brings the human being to the level of perfection, and brings him to the Pleasure of Allāh, and raises his status.

The Sayings of the Prophet

Verily, We have sent you (O Muhammad Peace be upon him) with the truth (Islam), a bringer of glad tidings (for those who believe in what you brought, that they will enter Paradise) and a warner (for those who disbelieve in what you brought, they will enter the Hell-fire). And you will not be asked about the dwellers of the blazing Fire. [2:119]

$$\text{إِنَّا أَرْسَلْنَاكَ بِالْحَقِّ بَشِيرًا وَنَذِيرًا ۖ وَلَا تُسْأَلُ عَنْ أَصْحَابِ الْجَحِيمِ ﴿١١٩﴾}$$

And with the help of Allāh, the Prophet, peace and blessings be upon him, sought to lead his nation to Paradise, the abode of peace and security. So, he spent nearly 23 years calling to the message of Islām that Allāh had tasked him with. He faced the horrors he faced for the sake of relaying his message – the message of Islām – in order to leave his nation on the clear path.

The Sayings of the Prophet

And among them are those who abuse the Prophet and say: "He is an ear." Say, "[It is] an ear of goodness for you that believes in Allah and believes the believers and [is] a mercy to those who believe among you." And those who abuse the Messenger of Allah - for them is a painful punishment. [9:61]

وَمِنْهُمُ ٱلَّذِينَ يُؤْذُونَ ٱلنَّبِيَّ وَيَقُولُونَ هُوَ أُذُنٌ قُلْ أُذُنُ خَيْرٍ لَّكُمْ يُؤْمِنُ بِٱللَّهِ وَيُؤْمِنُ لِلْمُؤْمِنِينَ وَرَحْمَةٌ لِّلَّذِينَ ءَامَنُوا۟ مِنكُمْ وَٱلَّذِينَ يُؤْذُونَ رَسُولَ ٱللَّهِ لَهُمْ عَذَابٌ أَلِيمٌ ﴿٦١﴾

If we look to the purpose of the message of Islām, we find that it can be summed up in the purifying and nourishing of the soul, and this takes place by knowing and worshipping Allāh, as well as strengthening the ties of brotherhood to spread justice between the slaves of Allāh.

The means of doing so is by implementing the teachings of our truthful Prophet, peace and blessings be upon him, which he gathered for us in the treasures and jewels of his Sunnah, his deep words, and what we call Islāmic law (Sharī'ah, or Fiqh).

The Sayings of the Prophet

Introduction

This book offers inspiring sayings of the Messenger of Allah, Muhammad, peace and blessings be upon him. The Prophet's sayings addresses many questions of importance:

- How can I change my life for the better?

- Is it considered worship to work every day in order to provide for my family?

- What is the proper and best manner in treating one's father, mother, sisters, brothers, neighbors, wife, and friends?

- What is the best and moderate way of worship?

- Can one be charitable despite being poor?

- What are the seven most destructive sins?

- Are the gates of forgiveness and happiness ever open to the sinner?

This book gives you answers from the authentic sayings of the Prophet, peace and blessings be upon him. It must be noted that the bulk of these sayings were taken from Sahīh Muslim and Sahih al-Bukhari. They are two of the most authentic and reliable sources of Prophetic sayings. The Prophet's sayings are arranged alphabetically by subject.

Altruism

1- "None of you [truly] believes until he wishes for his brother what he wishes for himself."

Arrogance

2- "A person shall not enter Paradise if he/she has, in their heart, a small atom's weight of arrogance. A man said: "One likes to wear beautiful clothes and nice shoes?" (meaning, is this considered arrogance?) The Prophet (pbuh) said: "God is beautiful and He likes beauty. Arrogance is to reject the truth, and despise other people."

Bedtime Prayer

3- "When you go to bed, say, 'O my God,

I submit my soul to You, and I turn my face to You, and I entrust my affairs to You, and I commit my burden to You, longing for You yet dreading You: there is no shelter from You, nor haven, except with You. I believe in Your Book, which You have revealed, and Your prophets, whom You have sent.' Then if you die that night, you will die in innocence; and if you wake up the next morning, you will encounter good."

Bribery

4- "The Prophet (pbuh) cursed the one who offers bribe, the one who receives it, and the one who arranges it."

Brotherhood

5- "The example of believers in relation to kindness, mercy, and sympathy they have for each other, is that of the body; when a limb of it aches, the whole body responds to it, with sleeplessness, and fever."

Characteristics of the hypocrite

6- "Whoever has the following four characteristics is a pure hypocrite. And whoever has one of the following four characteristics will have one of the characteristics of hypocrisy: Whenever he is entrusted, he betrays. Whenever he speaks, he lies. Whenever he makes a promise, he breaks it. And whenever he argues he behaves very badly."

Charity

You do not have to be rich to be charitable

7- Some poor Muslims complained to the Prophet (pbuh), saying: 'The affluent have made off with all the rewards: they pray as we pray, fast as we fast, and give away in charity from their money, while we are poor.' The Prophet (pbuh) said: 'Has not God made things for you to give away in charity? Every *tasbīhah*[2] is charity, every *takbīrah*[3] is charity, every *tahmīdah*[4] is charity, and every *tahlīlah*[5] is charity, to enjoin good and forbid evil is charity.' They said: 'One satisfies his sexual desire and is rewarded for it?' He said: 'Do you not think that if he were to satisfy his desire unlawfully he would be sinning? Likewise, if he satisfies his desire lawfully, he will have a reward for doing so.'

8- "Acting justly between two people is charity; helping a man in riding his animal, or in lifting his provisions to the back of the animal is charity: a good word is charity, every step you take to prayer is charity and removing a harmful thing from the road is charity too."

9- "Do not belittle any act of kindness. Therefore, meeting your brother with a cheerful face is considered charity."

10- "There is no Muslim who grows a plant or sows a seed, then birds, or a human being, or an animal eat of it, but it is charity for him."

11- "When a Muslim plants a plant, anything eaten of it or stolen from it is accounted as charity for him."

Command the right and forbid the evil

12- "Whosoever of you sees an evil action, let him change it with his hand. If he is not able to do so, then with his tongue; and if he is not able to do so, then with his heart; and that is the weakest of faith."

Contentment

13- "Whoever, at the start of the day, has no worries concerning safety and security, with a healthy body and a means of a day-to-day livelihood is [blessed with something great] just like the one to whom the entire world has been given."

Courtesy

14- "A young man never honours an old man due to age but that God sends someone to honour him when he reaches that age."

15- "He is not one of us who does not show compassion to our little one and recognize the rights of our elders."

Daughters

16- "Whoever has three daughters and, in addition to being patient with them, provides them with food, drink as well as clothes, he will be shielded from Fire because of them."

Death

17- "When someone dies, he is completely cut off from this world in the hereafter except for three things (whose blessings shall reach him): a perpetual charity, useful knowledge that others continue to benefit from; and a pious son praying for him."

18- "During the funeral, three things follow the dead person: his family members; his property; and his works. The first and the second return, while the third remains."

Disease

19- "God has sent down the disease and the

cure, and for every disease there is a cure. So take medicine but do not use anything unlawful as medicine."

Do not wait
20- "Undertake good works before you are overtaken by one of seven misfortunes: distracting poverty, corrupting wealth, debilitating illness, befuddling senility, final death, the Antichrist, the worst coming absent to wait for, or the final hour, which is more calamitous and more painful."

Easiness
21- "A man from among those who were before you was called to account. Nothing in the way of good was found for him

except that he used to have dealings with people and, being well-to-do, he would order his servants to let off the man suffering from a financial burden (so he could not repay his debt). Then, the Prophet (pbuh) said that God said: 'We are worthier than you of that (of being so generous). Let him off.'"

Equality

22- "O people! Verily, your Lord is One, and your father (Adam) is one. There is no superiority for an Arab over a non-Arab, neither a black over a white, or a white over a black except in piety and righteousness."

23- A noble woman belonging to the tribe of Makhzum was found guilty of theft.

Therefore, according to the law, the Prophetb (pbuh) had decided to have her hand cut off. Her relations requested Usamah Ibn Zayd, for whom the Prophet (pbuh) respected and loved so much, to intercede for her, so that she may be released. The Prophet (pbuh) said to Usamah, 'Do you intercede concerning punishments prescribed by God.' Then the Prophet (pbuh) delivered a sermon saying, 'Nations before you met their destruction because when the sons of nobility stole, they acquitted them, but when the poor and the weak stole, they punished them. By God, if Fatimah, my daughter, steals, I will cut off her hand.' *[see a note about the penalty for theft crime, p59]*

Ethics of *Jihād*

24- The Prophet (pbuh), in all battles, used to instruct the Muslim army to be aware of the following: "Go to war in adherence to the religion of God, do not kill children, avoid touching people who devoted themselves to worship in hermitages, never murder women and the elderly, do not set trees on fire or cut them down, never destroy houses, do not mutilate, do not deceive. "

Five Duties

25- "A Muslim has five duties towards another Muslim; to return a salutation, visit the sick, follow funerals, accept an invitation and say 'God have mercy on you' when one sneezes."

Forbearance

26- "May the mercy of God be on one who is kind and forbearing when he sells, kind and forbearing when he buys, kind and forbearing when he makes a demand."

27- One a bedouin urinated in the mosque. So, Companions rushed to beat him. The Prophet (pbuh) asked them to leave him alone, to let him finish and to pour water over the place where he has passed urine. Then, the Prophet gently and calmly explained to the bedouin that the mosque is a place of worship. After the bedouin had left, the Prophet (pbuh) said to his companions, 'You ought to make things easy, not difficult, for the people.'

Forgiveness

28- "Your Lord says: 'O son of Adam, so long as you call upon Me and ask of Me, I shall forgive you for what you have done, and I shall not mind. O son of Adam, were your sins to reach the clouds of the sky and were you then to ask forgiveness of Me, I would forgive you. O son of Adam, Were you to come to me with sins nearly as great as the earth and were you then to face Me (in sincere repentance) ascribing no partner to Me, I would bring you forgiveness nearly as great as the earth.'"

29- "Our Lord descends each night to the earth's sky when there remains the final third of the night, and He says, 'Who is saying a prayer to Me that I may answer it? Who is asking something of Me that I may give it to him? Who is asking forgiveness of Me that I may forgive him?'"

30- "A man sinned greatly against himself, and when death came to him he charged his sons, saying: 'When I have died, burn me, then crush me and scatter my ashes into the sea, for, by God, if my Lord takes possession of me, He will punish me in a manner in which He has punished no one else.' So they did that to him. Then God said to the earth: 'Produce what you have taken, and there he was!' And God said to him: 'What induced you to do what you did?' He said: 'Being afraid of You, O my Lord' and because of that He forgave him.'"

Gentleness

31- "Gentleness never accompanies anything without enhancing it, nor is it ever removed from anything without demeaning it."

Gift

32- "Exchange gifts, and mutual love arises; shake hands, and enmity will fall away."

God, the Almighty

33- Among the sayings that the Prophet attributes to his Lord is that God said: "The son of Adam denied Me and he had no right to do so. And he reviled Me and he had no right to do so. As for his denying Me, it is his saying: He will not remake me as He made me at first,[6] and the initial creation [of him] is no easier for Me than remaking him. As for his reviling Me, it is his saying: God has taken to Himself a son, while I am the One, the Everlasting Refuge. I begot not nor was I begotten, and there is none comparable to Me."

34- Another saying attributed to God runs as follows: "O My servants, I have forbidden oppression for Myself and have made it forbidden amongst you, so do not oppress one another. O My servants, all of you are astray except for those I have guided, so seek guidance of Me and I shall guide you, O My servants, all of you are hungry except for those I have fed, so seek food of Me and I shall feed you. O My servants, all of you are naked except for those I have clothed, so seek clothing of Me and I shall clothe you. O My servants, you sin by night and by day, and I forgive all sins, so seek forgiveness of Me and I shall forgive you. O My servants, you will not attain harming Me so as to harm Me, and will not attain benefitting Me so as to benefit Me. O My servants, were the first of you and the last of you, the human of you and the jinn of you to be as pious as the most pious heart of any one man of you, that would not increase My kingdom in anything. O My servants, were the first of you and the last of you, the human of you and the jinn of you to be as wicked as the most wicked heart of any one man of you, that would not decrease My kingdom in anything. O My servants, were the first of you and the last of you, the human of you and the jinn of you to rise up in one place and make a request of Me, and were I to give everyone what he requested, that would not decrease what I have, any more that a needle decreases the sea if put into it. O My servants, it is but your deeds that I reckon up for you and then recompense you for, so let him finds good praise Allah and let him who finds other that blame no one but himself."

Good deeds & bad deeds

35- "He who has intended a good deed and has not done it, God writes it down with Himself as a full good deed, but if he has intended it and has done it, God writes it down for Himself as from ten good deeds to seven hundred times, or many times over. But if he has intended a bad deed and has not done it, God writes it down with Himself as a full good deed, but if he has intended it and has done it, God writes it down as one bad deed."

Grudge

36- "The doors of Paradise are opened on Mondays and Thursdays. Every one who does not associate anything with God will be forgiven, except for the one who bears a grudge against his brother. It is said, 'Wait for these two until they reconcile, wait for these two until they reconcile, wait for these two until they reconcile.'"

Heart is the king of the body

37- "Truly in the body there is a morsel of flesh which, if it be whole, all the body is whole and which, if it be diseased, all of it is diseased. Truly it is the heart."

Help

38- "Whosoever removes a worldly grief from a believer, God will remove from him one of the griefs of the Day of Judgment. Whosoever alleviates the lot of a needy person, God will alleviate his lot in this world and the world to come."

39- "Help your brother, whether he be an oppressor or one of the oppressed. Some said, 'O Messenger of God, we help him if he is oppressed; but how can we help him if he is an oppressor?' The Prophet (pbuh) said, 'By stopping him from oppression."

Hoarding

40- "Any one who withholds goods until prices rise, he is held to be a sinner."

Intelligence & Incompetence

41- "The intelligent one is the one who holds himself responsible and works for what which is after death. And the incompetent one is the one who indulges himself in pursuit of personal desire and importunes God."

Judge

42- "There are three classes of judges; one of

whom will be in the Garden while other two will be in Hell-Fire. The one who will be in the Garden is a man who knew the truth and judged accordingly. The one who knew the truth but misjudged and the one who judged for the people in ignorance will be both in Hell-Fire."

Justice

43- "The just will be on platforms of light in the presence of God; those who are just in their decisions, with their families, and with what they are in charge of."

Kindness

44- "Verily, God is kind, and likes kindness in all affairs."

Kinship

45- "Whoever would be glad to have his livelihood expanded and his life prolonged should maintain family ties."

Knowledge

46- "Whosoever follows a path to seek knowledge therein, God will make easy for him a path to Paradise."

47- "Acquiring knowledge is binding upon every Muslim."

48- "He who goes out in search of knowledge is in God's path till he returns."

Merchant

49- "An honest and trustworthy merchant

will be in heaven, associated with the prophets, the upright, and the martyrs."

Mercy

50- "When God created His creation, He pledged Himself in His book: My mercy prevails over My anger."

51- "The merciful are granted mercy by God. Show mercy to those on earth so that you are shown mercy by the One in Heaven."

52- "When God created the heavens and earth, He created one hundred mercies; each of them filled the space between the heavens and earth. He placed one mercy on earth. It is through this that a mother is compassionate to her baby, and so are wild beasts and birds. On the Day of Judgment, God will complement them with this one mercy."

Mercy extended to animals

53- "Once a prostitute had seen a dog walking to and fro in front of a well on a very hot day. His tongue was hanging out because of his thirst. She used her shoe to give him water to drink. So, God forgave her because of her mercy."

54- "Whoever kills a sparrow or anything bigger than that without a just cause, God will hold him accountable on the Day of Judgement. The listeners asked, 'O Prophet, what is a just cause?' He replied that he will kill it to eat it, not simply to chop off its head and then throw it away."

Moderation

Food and drink

55- "There is no worse vessel for the son of Adam to fill than his own stomach. But if he must fill it, then let him allow one third for food, one third for drink, and one third for air."

Worship

56- Once, three people came to the home of the Prophet (pbuh), enquiring of his wives about his worship. When they were told of it, they felt that it was less than expected. Then one of them said, 'How can we compare ourselves to God's Messenger when God has already forgiven him any sin that he might have committed and any which he may commit in the future.' Hence, one of them declared, 'I shall spend all the night, every night, in prayer.' The second said, 'As for me, I shall fast every day of my life.' The third one said, 'I shall stay away from women and will never get married.' The Prophet (pbuh) went to them and said, 'Are you the ones who said so and so. You should know that I am the one who fears God most among you. Nevertheless, I fast on some days, and abstain from fasting on others; I pray, but I also go to sleep; and I get married. Whoever abandons my path does not belong to me.'

Morals

57- "The best of you are those who have the best morals."

Mother

58- A young man asked the Prophet (pbuh): 'Who of all people is most worthy of my kindness?' The Prophet (pbuh) answered, 'Your mother.' The man asked: 'And then who?' The Prophet (pbuh) answered, 'Your mother.' The man asked again: 'And then who?' The Prophet (pbuh) answered, 'Your mother.' The man asked yet again: 'And then who?' answered, 'Your father.' The Prophet (pbuh) said.

Neighbourhood

59- "Whosoever believes in God and the Last

Day let him be kind to his neighbour."

60- "Angel Gabriel would frequently advise me to take care of my neighbour until thought that he [i.e. Gabriel] would make him an inheritor."

61- "Whosoever believes in God, and the last Day, he must not cause harm to his neighbour."

62- "He is not a perfect believer, the one who sleeps on a full stomach, while he knows that his neighbour is hungry."

Non-Muslims

63- "On the day of Resurrection I shall dispute with any one who oppresses a *Muʿāhid* (a non-Muslim granted, for a certain period of time, the pledge of protection by Muslims), or violates his right, or puts a responsibility on him which is beyond his strength, or takes something from him against his will."

64- "Whoever killed a *dhimmi* (a non-Muslim citizen, mainly of the people of the Book who is subject to poll tax, in return for Muslim protection) shall not smell the fragrance of Paradise though its fragrance can be smelt at a distance of forty years (of travelling)."

Prayer (du'ā')
65- "God would not like to see His servant holding out his arms pleading for help and turn him away empty handed."

66- "Prayers shall be answered unless one asks for something evil or the break-up of kinship relations, and as long as one does not become impatient." When the Prophet(pbuh) was asked to explain how one becomes impatient, he said: 'One says, 'I have prayed many times but I have had no response, then he gives up hope and abandons Prayer altogether."

67- "Prayers by three people shall never be turned down: a just ruler; a fasting person until he breaks the fast; and the oppressed for whose prayer the gates of heaven shall be opened wide and God shall say to him, 'By My power, I shall support you, even though it may be in due course.'"

Prophets

68- "The parable of me and of previous prophets is that of a man who built a house excellently and completely, apart from the space of one brick which he did not put. The people started to walk around the building, admiring it and saying, 'If only that brick were put in its place.' I have come to complete that brick, and I am the seal of the prophets."

69- "All the prophets are paternal brothers, even though their mothers are different."

Quarrelsomeness

70- "The most odious of men to God is the one who is most quarrelsome."

Sincerity

71- "The first of people against whom judgment will be pronounced on the Day of Resurrection will be a man who died a martyr. He will be brought and God will make known to him His favours and he will recognize them. God will say: 'What did you do about them?' He will say: 'I fought for you until I died a martyr.' He will say: 'You have lied; you fought that it might be said of you: 'He is courageous.' And so it was said.' Then he will be ordered to be dragged along on his face until he is cast into Hell-fire. Another will be a man who has studied religious knowledge and has taught it and who used to recite the Qur'ān. He will be brought and God will make known to him

His favours and he will recognize them. God will say: 'what did you do about them?' He will say: 'I studied religious knowledge and I taught it and I recited the Qur'ān for Your sake.' God will say: 'You have lied; you did but study religious knowledge that it might be said of you: 'He is learned.' And you recited the Qur'ān that it might be said of you: 'He is a reciter.' And so it was said.' Then he will be ordered to be dragged along on his face until he is cast into Hell-fire. Another will be a man whom God had made rich and to whom He had given all kinds of wealth. He will be brought and God will make known to him His favours and he will recognize them. God will say: 'What did you do about them?

He will say: 'I left no way in which You like money to be spent without spending in it for Your sake.' God will say: 'You have lied; you did but do so that it might be said of you: 'He is open-handed.' And so it was said.' Then he will be ordered to be dragged along on his face until he is cast into Hell-fire."

Suicide

72- "He who throws himself down from a rock and commits suicide will throw himself into Hell-fire; he who drinks poison and kills himself will have the poison in his hand, drinking it forever in Hell-fire; and he who kills himself with a weapon will have that weapon in his hand, stabbing himself forever in Hell-fire."

Test & Trial

73- "How amazing the affairs of the believer are, because there is good for him in all his affairs. If he receives a good thing, he is grateful (to his Lord), and this is good for him, while if he is struck with adversity, he is patient and it is good for him."

The bankrupt

74- "Do you know the one who is bankrupt?" They said, 'The bankrupt is the one who has neither money nor possessions.' The Prophet (pbuh) said, 'The real bankrupt is the one who, on the Day of Resurrection, comes with prayers, fasting and Zakat[7] (to his credit), but he also insulted this one, slandered that one, devoured the one's wealth, shed the blood of another, and beaten another. So they will be given some of his good deeds (as compensation). If his good deeds run out before all of them take their rights back, some of their sins will be taken and cast onto him, then he will be cast into Hell-Fire."

The influence of association

75- "Good companions and bad companions are like sellers of musk and the furnace of the blacksmith. You lose nothing from the musk seller, whether you buy some or smell or are imbued with its fragrance. The furnace of the blacksmith, on the other hand, burns your clothes, or you get a noxious odor"

76- "A man inclines to the belief of his friend, so let each one of you watch out who he befriends."

The seven great destructive sins

77- "Avoid the seven great destructive things. People asked, 'What are they?' The Prophet (pbuh) said, 'Idolatry; sorcery; killing a person declared inviolable by God, except for a just reason; devouring usury; consuming the property of an orphan; running away from battle; and falsely accusing chaste believing women of adultery."

The seven fortunate people

78- "Seven people are sheltered by the shade of God on the Day of Judgment, when there is no shade but His: a just ruler; a youth raised in obedience to God; a man whose heart is devoted to mosques; two brothers (or sisters) whose fraternity is for God; a young man whom a woman of beauty attempted to seduce but he replied, 'I fear God;' a man who gave charity in silence so that his left hand did not know what his right had spent; a person who remembered God in his privacy and tears flooded his eyes."

Tolerance

79- "Once a funeral procession passed by the Prophet (pbuh). [As a gesture of respect] he rose. Thereupon someone remarked, 'O Messenger of God, it is a funeral of a Jew.' He replied: 'Is it not a soul?!"

Truth

80- "Tell the truth even if it be unpleasant"

81- "The best form of *jihad* is to tell a word of truth to an oppressive ruler."

Trust in God

82- "If you really trusted in God as God should be trusted, He would sustain you as He sustains the birds. They go out in the morning hungry, and come back to rest in the evening full."

Wife

83- "The best of you are those who are the

most kind to their wives. And I am the best amongst you in this respect."

84- "A believer must not hate his wife. If he is displeased with one bad quality in her, then let him be pleased with one that is good in her."

Wine

85- "Keep away from wine, for it is the mother of evil."

Various issues and instructions

86- "Do not envy one another; do not inflate prices one to another; do not hate one another; do not turn away from one another; and do not undercut one another, but be you, O servants of

God, brothers. A Muslim is the brother of a Muslim: he neither oppresses him nor does he fail him, nor does he lie to him, nor does he hold him in contempt. Piety is right here-and he (the Prophet) pointed to his chest three times. It is evil enough for a man to hold his brother Muslim in contempt. The whole affairs of a Muslim for another Muslim are inviolable: his blood, his property, and his honor."

87- "None of you truly believes until he wishes for his brother what he wishes for himself."

88- "Health and leisure are two blessings which many people do not appreciate."

89- "A believer is not abusive, nor is he a slanderer, nor does he curse."

90- "If a man works for his aged parents, that is in the path of God; if he works for his young children, that is in the path of God; if he works for himself, to be free of want, that is in the path of God."

91- "Hearts [from time to time] get rusty. When was asked about their polish, he said: 'Recitation of the Qur'ān.'"

92- "Once a man, who was passing through a road, found a branch of a tree with thorns obstructing it. The man removed the thorns from the way. Allah thanked him and forgave his sins."

93- "It is not permissible for a Muslim to be estranged from his brother for more than three days, both of them turning away from one another when they meet. The better of them is the one who is first to greet the other."

94- "An ant bit one of the earlier prophets, so he ordered the ant dwellings to be burnt. Through inspiration God asked him: 'If you are bitten by an ant, would you burn a whole nation which glorifies God?'"

95- "Let him who believes in God and the Last Day either speak good or keep silent."

96- "The example of those who faithfully abide by God's commandments and those who do not is like a group of travellers who shared a ship, some on the upper deck and some below. When the latter needed water, they had to go up to bring it, so they said: 'Let us make a hole in our part of the ship (to get water) directly.' But if those on the upper deck allow them to do what they had suggested, all of them will be destroyed, while if they prevent them from doing so, all of them will be safe."

97- "The strong person is not the one who is good at wrestling. The strong person is the one who controls himself when angry."

98- "God does not look at your bodies and figures, but looks at your hearts and your deeds."

99- "Eat together and not separately, for blessing is associated with the company."

100- "Be mindful of God, you will find Him before you. Get to know God in ease and God will acknowledge you in distress. And know that help comes with patience, and that relief comes with distress; and that with difficulty comes ease."

Love is ...

Sending blessing upon Prophet Muhammad Peace be Upon Him

Note on the penalty for theft crime

'By God, if Fatimah, my daughter, steals, I will cut off her hand.' (The Prophetic saying, no. 22). It is likely for the westerner to get offended by this sentence that runs quite contrary to Western norms and principles.

I shall, in passing, give an explanation. Islam has set up fixed, mandatory punishments, based on the Qur'ān and Prophetic *Sunnah*, for certain crimes (theft, banditry, adultery, an unfounded accusation of adultery, the drinking of alcohol, apostasy). The principal purpose of these fixed punishments is deterrence from acts that are harmful to humanity, for the more such serious crimes prevail, the more fatal consequences on a large scale they produce.

It maybe argued that these fixed punishments are very harsh and heavy. On the surface, this could be a valid argument. But on a deeper level, one may come to an opposite vision. For example, according to the law, the fixed penalty for theft is the amputation of the right hand. If someone, not driven by starvation or any pressing need, thinks of stealing, being aware of the severe punishment for it, he would reconsider his decision countless times before committing this crime, since he well knows that he shall pay the price very dearly, if he is caught and proven guilty. He will cause his right hand to be cut off. A very high price indeed! Actually, he would relinquish the mere thought of stealing altogether. This penalty, as well as other penalties, ultimately brings about a mercy for the individual and the community, through preventing them from acting any crime that might do serious harm to them. These penalties are, to a large extent, meant to act as 'preventive measures,' giving a pre-warning to people not to get near, let alone all kinds of involvements, to certain areas whose harm shall permeate various levels of the society.

On the other hand, it is interesting to note that some of the fixed punishments are applicable in theory, while in practice unenforceable.

For example, the requirements needed to apply the penalty for adultery crime are either four eyewitnesses to testify that they have seen the offence, or a confession made four times in four different sessions. One easily notices that this penalty, based on such quite rarely existent conditions, is impossible to occur. Typically, no one testifies against himself four times in four different sessions that he committed adultery. This clearly proves that the fixed punishments have more to do with prevention, and caution, and a little to do with application and enforcement.

Moreover, Islam encourages the victim to pardon and forgive the offender, so potential penalty would be somehow prevented. The Prophet (pbuh) says, 'Spare the enforcement of the fixed punishments wherever possible. If there is any way out for the accused, let him go unpunished.' This in very brief might give some proper knowledge of the Islamic criminal law.

Is the penalty for theft applicable in all cases? Are there any restrictions on it?

Theft, as defined by Islamic law, is 'surreptitiously taking away of movable property with a certain minimum value which is not partially owned by the thief nor entrusted to him, from a place which is locked or under guard.'

There are several special circumstances, only by which the penalty for the theft is to be enforced.

1- The thief must be adult, and sane; he was not forced to steal.

2- The act must have been surreptitious. If someone steals goods from a market stall in broad daylight, the penalty for theft cannot be imposed, because the goods were not stolen surreptitiously.

3- The value of the stolen goods must reach a minimum limit, below which the penalty is not enforced. The minimum limit according to some jurists is 1.06 g of gold (one-quarter of a gold dinar of 4.25g) or 29.7g of silver (10 dirhams) according to others.

4- The goods must be capable of being owned. Therefore, the kidnapping of a free person does not entail the penalty, since free persons cannot be owned.

5- The goods must have legal values. Some

goods, like wine and pigs are legally of no value, because they are impure and forbidden. Thus a non-Muslim can own them, but not a Muslim. As a consequence, the penalty can only be enforced if such goods are stolen from a non-Muslim.

6- A further requirement for the penalty is that the thief must not have the goods legally at his disposal or be a co-owner. For example, a shop assistant who takes away goods or money from the shop he attends to, or a person who steals state property, or a solider who steals from the war booty that has not yet been divided cannot be punished with amputation.

7- The stolen goods must have been guarded

or stored in an adequate place. Locked houses, shops, stables, and coffers count as such places, taking into account the nature of the object. A stable, for instance, is a suitable place for cattle, but not for jewelry. The stealing of a horse left in front of a mosque or of a thing found in a public bath does not qualify as legal theft.

8- The application of the fixed punishment for the theft is further restricted by doubt and uncertainty (*Shubhah*) as to the unlawfulness of the act. For instance, if a person steals from his son or wife, or debtor, no penalty is imposed. The same applies when it is proven that the thief stole food to eat because of hunger.

Finally, Islam is keen not to enforce the punishment when a slight doubt exists. The Prophet (pbuh) said, 'Block the enforcement of prescribed punishments in any case of doubt.'

[See the above requirements in Peters, Rudolph. *Crime and Punishment in Islamic Law*. (Cambridge: Cambridge University Press, 2005) p 56, and Ibn Naqib, *Reliance of the Traveller*. Translated by Nuh Ha Mim Keller. (USA: Amana publications, 1994) p613-614].

٩٩- قَالَ رَسُولُ اللهِ صَلَّى اللهُ عَلَيْهِ وَسَلَّمَ: «كُلُوا جَمِيعًا وَلَا تَفَرَّقُوا فَإِنَّ الْبَرَكَةَ مَعَ الْجَمَاعَةِ».

١٠٠- قَالَ رَسُولُ اللهِ صَلَّى اللهُ عَلَيْهِ وَسَلَّمَ: «تَعَرَّفْ إلى اللهِ في الرَّخاءِ يَعْرِفْكَ في الشدة. واعلمْ أن النصر مع الصبر، و أن الفرج مع الكرب، وأن مع العسر يسرا، ولن يغلب عُسْرٌ يُسْرَينِ».

Love is ...

Sending blessing upon Prophet Muhammad Peace be Upon Him

٩٥- قَالَ رَسُولُ اللَّهِ صَلَّى اللَّهُ عَلَيْهِ وَسَلَّمَ: «من كان يُؤمن بالله واليوم الآخر فَلْيَقُلْ خيرا أو لِيَصْمُتْ».

٩٦- قَالَ رَسُولُ اللَّهِ صَلَّى اللَّهُ عَلَيْهِ وَسَلَّمَ: «مَثَلُ القائم في حُدُودِ اللَّهِ والْوَاقِعِ فيها، كَمَثَلِ قوم اسْتَهَموا على سَفينَةٍ، فَأَصَابَ بَعْضُهُم أَعْلَاهَا، وبعضُهم أَسْفَلَهَا، فكان الذي في أسفلها إذا اسْتَقَوْا من الماء مَرُّوا على مَنْ فَوقَهمْ، فقالوا: لو أنا خَرَقْنا في نَصِيبنا خرقا وَلَمْ نُؤذِ مَنْ فَوقَنا ؟ فإن تَرَكُوهُمْ وما أَرَادوا هَلَكوا وهلكوا جَميعا، وإنْ أخذُوا على أيدِيهِمْ نَجَوْا ونَجَوْا جَميعا».

٩٧- قَالَ رَسُولُ اللَّهِ صَلَّى اللَّهُ عَلَيْهِ وَسَلَّمَ: «المؤمن القويُّ خيرٌ وأحبُّ إلى الله من المؤمن الضعيف، وفي كلِّ خيرٌ».

٩٨- قَالَ رَسُولُ اللَّهِ صَلَّى اللَّهُ عَلَيْهِ وَسَلَّمَ: «إن الله لا ينظر إلى أجسادكم، ولا إلى صُوَرِكم، ولكن ينظر إلى قلوبكم وأعمالكم».

٩١- قَالَ رَسُولُ اللَّهِ صَلَّى اللَّهُ عَلَيْهِ وَسَلَّمَ: «إنَّ هذه القُلوبَ تَصْدأ كما يَصْدأ الحديدُ»، قيل: فما جَلاؤها يا رسول الله؟ قال: «تلاوةُ القرآن».

٩٢- قَالَ رَسُولُ اللَّهِ صَلَّى اللَّهُ عَلَيْهِ وَسَلَّمَ: «بينما رجلٌ يمشي بطريقٍ وجَدَ غُصْنَ شَوْكٍ على الطريق، فأخَّرَهُ، فشَكَرَ اللهُ له، فغَفَرَ له».

٩٣- قَالَ رَسُولُ اللَّهِ صَلَّى اللَّهُ عَلَيْهِ وَسَلَّمَ: «لا يَحِلُّ لمسلمٍ أن يهجرَ أخاه فوقَ ثلاثِ ليالٍ، يلتقيان، فيُعرِضُ هذا، ويُعرِضُ هذا، وخيرُهما الذي يبدأُ بالسلام».

٩٤- قَالَ رَسُولُ اللَّهِ صَلَّى اللَّهُ عَلَيْهِ وَسَلَّمَ: «قَرَصَت نملةٌ نبيّاً من الأنبياء، فأمرَ بقريةِ النَّملِ فأُحْرِقَت، فأوحى اللهُ إليهِ: أنْ قَرَصَتْكَ نملةٌ أحْرَقْتَ أُمَّةً مِن الأُمَمِ تُسَبِّحُ؟».

٨٧- قال رَسولُ اللهِ صَلَّى اللهُ عَلَيْهِ وَسَلَّمَ: «لا يُؤمِنُ أحدُكُمْ حتَّى يُحِبَّ لأخيه ما يُحِبُّ لنفسه».

٨٨- قال رَسولُ اللهِ صَلَّى اللهُ عَلَيْهِ وَسَلَّمَ: «نعمتان مَغْبُون فيهما كثير من الناس: الصحة، والفراغ».

٨٩- قَالَ رَسولُ اللهِ صَلَّى اللهُ عَلَيْهِ وَسَلَّمَ: «لَيْسَ الْمُؤْمِنُ بِالطَّعَّانِ وَلَا اللَّعَّانِ وَلَا الْفَاحِشِ وَلَا الْبَذِيءِ».

٩٠- [مَرَّ عَلَى النَّبِيِّ صَلَّى اللهُ عَلَيْهِ وَسَلَّمَ رَجُلٌ، فَرَأى أَصْحَابُ رَسُولِ اللهِ صَلَّى اللهُ عَلَيْهِ وَسَلَّمَ مِنْ جَلْدِهِ وَنَشَاطِهِ، فَقَالُوا: يَا رَسُولَ اللهِ: لَوْ كَانَ هَذَا فِي سَبِيلِ اللهِ؟،] فَقَالَ رَسُولُ اللهِ صَلَّى اللهُ عَلَيْهِ وَسَلَّمَ: «إِنْ كَانَ يَسْعَى على أَبَوَيْنِ شَيْخَيْنِ كَبِيرَيْنِ فَهُوَ فِي سَبِيلِ اللهِ، إِوِنْ كَانَ خَرَجَ يَسْعَى عَلَى وَلَدِهِ صِغَارًا فَهُوَ فِي سَبِيلِ اللهِ، وَإِنْ كَانَ يَسْعَى عَلَى نَفْسِهِ لِيُعِفَّهَا فَهُوَ فِي سَبِيلِ اللهِ».

٨٣- قَالَ رَسُولُ اللهِ صَلَّى اللهُ عَلَيْهِ وَسَلَّمَ: «خيرُكم خيرُكم لأهْلِهِ، وأنا خيرُكم لأهْلي».

٨٤- قَالَ رَسُولُ اللهِ صَلَّى اللهُ عَلَيْهِ وَسَلَّمَ: «لَا يَفْرَكْ مُؤْمِنٌ مُؤْمِنَةً إنْ كَرِهَ مِنْهَا خُلُقًا، رَضِيَ مِنْهَا آخَرَ».

٨٥- قال رَسُولُ اللهِ صَلَّى اللهُ عَلَيْهِ وَسَلَّمَ: «اجْتَنِبُوا الخمرَ، فإنها أم الخَبَائِث».

٨٦- قال رَسُولُ اللهِ صَلَّى اللهُ عَلَيْهِ وَسَلَّمَ: «لا تَحاسَدوا، ولا تَنَاجَشوا، ولا تَبَاغَضُوا، ولا تدابَرُوا، ولا يَبِعْ بعضكم على بَيْعِ بعض، وكونوا عبادَ اللهِ إخوانا، المسلمُ أخو المسلم، لا يَظْلِمُهُ، ولا يَخْذُلُهُ، ولا يَحْقِرهُ، التقوى ها هنا - ويشير إلى صدره ثلاث مرات - بِحَسْبِ امرئ من الشَّرِّ: أن يَحْقِرَ أخاه المسلم، كلُّ المسلم على المسلم حرام: دمُه، ومالُه، وعِرْضُه».

ورجلان تحابًا في الله، اجتمعا على ذلك وتفرّقا عليه، ورجل دعتْهُ امرأة ذاتُ مَنْصِب وجمال، فقال: إني أخافُ الله، ورجل تصدَّق بصدقة فأخْفاها حتى لا تعلم شمالُهُ ما تُنْفِقُ يمينه، ورجل ذكَر الله خاليا ففاضت عيناه».

٧٩- مَرَّتْ بالنَّبِيِّ صَلَّى اللهُ عَلَيْهِ وَسَلَّمَ جِنَازَةٌ فقَامَ، فقِيلَ لَهُ: إنَّها جِنَازَةُ يَهُودِيٍّ فقَالَ أَلَيْسَتْ نَفْسًا.

٨٠- قَالَ رَسُولُ اللهِ صَلَّى اللهُ عَلَيْهِ وَسَلَّمَ: «قلِ الحقَّ، وإنْ كان مُرّاً».

٨١- قَالَ رَسُولُ اللهِ صَلَّى اللهُ عَلَيْهِ وَسَلَّمَ: «فضلُ الجهاد كلمة عدلٍ عند سُلطان جائرٍ».

٨٢- قَالَ رَسُولُ اللهِ صَلَّى اللهُ عَلَيْهِ وَسَلَّمَ: «لو أنَّكم كنتم تتوكلون على الله حقَّ توكله: لَرُزِقْتُم كما تُرزق الطَّيرُ، تَغدو خِماصا وتَروحُ بِطانا».

٧٥-قَالَ رَسُولُ اللهِ صَلَّى اللهُ عَلَيْهِ وَسَلَّمَ: «إِنَّمَا مَثَلُ الجليسِ الصالحُ والجليسُ السوءِ كحاملِ المسكِ، ونافخِ الكِيْرِ، فحاملُ المسكِ: إما أن يُحْذِيَكَ، وإما أن تبتاع منه، وإمَّا أن تجِدَ منه ريحًا طيِّبة، ونافخُ الكير: إما أن يَحرِقَ ثِيَابَكَ، وإما أن تجد منه ريحًا خبيثَة».

٧٦-قَالَ رَسُولُ اللهِ صَلَّى اللهُ عَلَيْهِ وَسَلَّمَ: «المرءُ على دينِ خليلِه، فلينظرْ أحدُكم مَن يُخَالِلْ».

٧٧-قَالَ رَسُولُ اللهِ صَلَّى اللهُ عَلَيْهِ وَسَلَّمَ: «اجتنبوا السبعَ الموبقاتِ، قيل: يا رسولَ الله، وما هُنَّ؟ قال: الشركُ بالله، والسِّحْرُ، وقتْلُ النفسِ التي حرَّم الله إلا بالحقِّ، وأكلُ مالِ اليتيمِ، وأكلُ الرِّبا، والتولي يومَ الزحفِ، وقذفُ المحصناتِ الغافلاتِ المؤمناتِ».

٧٨-قَالَ رَسُولُ اللهِ صَلَّى اللهُ عَلَيْهِ وَسَلَّمَ: «سَبْعَةٌ يظِلُّهُمُ اللهُ في ظِلِّهِ يومَ لا ظِلَّ إلا ظِلُّهُ: الإمامُ العادلُ، وشابٌّ نشأ في عبادةِ اللهِ عزَّ وجلَّ، ورجلٌ قلبُه مُعَلَّقٌ بالمسجدِ، إذا خرج منه حتى يعودَ إليه،

نَفسَه، فهو في نار جهنم يتردَّى فيها، خالدا مُخلَّدا فيها أبدا، وَمَنْ تَحَسَّى سُمَّا فقتلَ نفسَهُ، فَسُمُّهُ في يده يتحَسَّاه في نار جهنم، خالدا مُخلَّدا فيها أبدا، ومَنْ قتل نفسَهُ بحديدَة، فحديدتُهُ في يده، يَتَوَجَّأُ بها في بطنه في نار جهنم خالدا مُخلَّدا فيها أبدا».

٧٣- قَالَ رَسُولُ اللهِ صَلَّى اللهُ عَلَيْهِ وَسَلَّمَ: «عَجَباً لأمر المؤمن! إنَّ أمرَه كُلَّه له خير، وليس ذلك لأحد إلا للمؤمن، إن أصابتْهُ سَرَّاءُ شكر، فكان خيراً له، وإن أصابتْهُ ضَرَّاءُ صَبَرَ، فكان خيراً له»

٧٤- قَالَ رَسُولُ اللهِ صَلَّى اللهُ عَلَيْهِ وَسَلَّمَ يوماً: «أتَدْرُونَ ما المُفْلِسُ؟ قالوا: المفْلِسُ فينا من لا درهم له ولا متاع. قال: إن المفْلِسَ مَنْ يأتي يوم القيامة بصلاة وصيام وزكاة، ويأتي قد شَتَمَ هذا، وقذفَ هذا، وأكل مال هذا، وسفك دم هذا، وضرب هذا، فيُعطى هذا من حسناته، وهذا من حسناته، فإن فَنِيَتْ حَسَناتُهُ قبل أن يُقْضى ما عليه، أُخِذَ من خطايهم فطُرِحَتْ عليه، ثم يُطْرَحُ في النار».

٧١-قَالَ رَسُولُ اللَّهِ صَلَّى اللَّهُ عَلَيْهِ وَسَلَّمَ: «إنَّ أولَ النَّاسِ يُقْضَى يومَ القيامةِ عليهِ : رجلٌ استُشْهِدَ، فأتيَ بهِ، فعَرَّفهُ نِعَمَهُ، فعرفها، قال : فما عملتَ فيها ؟ قال : قاتلتُ فيكَ حتى استُشْهِدتُ، فقال : كذبتَ، ولكنك قاتلتَ لأن يقالَ : جَريءٌ، فقد قيلَ، ثم أُمِرَ بهِ، فَسُحِبَ على وَجهِهِ، حتى ألقيَ في النَّارِ. ورجلٌ تَعَلَّمَ العِلمَ وَعَلَّمَهُ، وقرأَ القرآنَ، فأُتِيَ بهِ، فعرَّفهُ نِعَمَهُ فعرفَها، قال: فما عملتَ فيها ؟ قال : تَعَلَّمْتُ العِلمَ وعلَّمتُهُ، وقرأتُ فيكَ القرآنَ، قال: كذبتَ، ولكنكَ تعلَّمتَ [العلم] ليقال: عالمٌ، وقرأتَ [القرآنَ] ليقال: [هو] قارئٌ، فقد قيل، ثُمَّ أُمِرَ بهِ، فَسُحِبَ على وجهِهِ، حتى ألقيَ في النَّارِ، ورجلٌ وسَّعَ اللهُ عليهِ، وأعطاهُ من أصنافِ المالِ [كُلِّهِ]، فأُتِيَ بهِ فعرَّفهَ نعمه، فعرفها، قال: فما عَمِلْتَ فيها؟ قال: ما تَرَكتُ من سبيلٍ تُحِبُّ أنْ يُنفَقَ فيها [إلا أنفقتُ فيها] لك، قال : كذبتَ، ولكنكَ فعلتَ لِيُقَالَ: هو جَوادٌ، فقد قيل، ثم أُمِرَ بهِ فَسُحِبَ على وجهِهِ ثم ألقيَ في النَّارِ».

٧٢-قَالَ رَسُولُ اللَّهِ صَلَّى اللَّهُ عَلَيْهِ وَسَلَّمَ: «مَن تَرَدَّى مِن جَبَلٍ فقتلَ

الإمامُ العادلُ، والصائم حين يفطِرُ، ودَعْوَة المظلوم يرفعها فوْقَ الغمام، وتُفْتَحُ لها أبوابُ السماء، ويقول الله تعالى: وعِزَّتي لأنْصُرنَّك ولو بعد حين».

٦٨-قَالَ رَسُولُ اللَّهِ صَلَّى اللَّهُ عَلَيْهِ وَسَلَّمَ: «إِنَّ مَثَلي وَمَثَلَ الأنبياءِ من قبلي، كمثل رجل بنى بُنْيَانا فأحْسَنَه وأجْمَلَه، إلا موضع لَبِنَة من زاوية من زواياه، فجعل الناسُ يطوفون به، ويَعْجَبون له، ويقولون: هلا وُضِعَتْ هذه اللَّبِنَةُ؟ قال: فأنا اللَّبِنَةُ، وأنا خَاتَمُ النَّبِيِّين».

٦٩-قَالَ رَسُولُ اللَّهِ صَلَّى اللَّهُ عَلَيْهِ وَسَلَّمَ: «الأنبياءُ إخْوَة، أبناءُ عَلَات، وأُمَّهَاتُهم شَتَّى».

٧٠-قَالَ رَسُولُ اللَّهِ صَلَّى اللَّهُ عَلَيْهِ وَسَلَّمَ: «إنَّ أبغض الرجالِ إلى اللهِ تَعَالَى: الأَلَدُّ الْخَصِمُ».

٦٣- قَالَ رَسُولُ اللهِ صَلَّى اللهُ عَلَيْهِ وَسَلَّمَ: «أَلَا مَنْ ظَلَمَ مُعَاهِدا، أو انتَقَصَهُ، أو كَلَّفَهُ فوقَ طاقَتِه، أَو أَخَذَ مِنهُ شَيئا بِغَيرِ طِيبِ نَفْسٍ، فأنا حَجِيجُهُ يومَ القِيامَةِ».

٦٤- قَالَ رَسُولُ اللهِ صَلَّى اللهُ عَلَيْهِ وَسَلَّمَ: «مَنْ قَتَلَ مُعَاهَدًا بِغَيْرِ حَقٍّ لَمْ يَرَحْ رَائِحَةَ الْجَنَّةِ وَإِنَّهُ لَيُوجَدُ رِيحُهَا مِنْ مَسِيرَةِ أَرْبَعِينَ عَامًا».

٦٥- قَالَ رَسُولُ اللهِ صَلَّى اللهُ عَلَيْهِ وَسَلَّمَ: «إنَّ اللهَ حَيِيٌّ كَرِيمٌ يَسْتَحْيِي مِنْ عَبْدِهِ إِذَا رَفَعَ يَدَيْهِ إِلَيْهِ أَنْ يَرُدَّهُمَا صِفْرًا».

٦٦- قَالَ رَسُولُ اللهِ صَلَّى اللهُ عَلَيْهِ وَسَلَّمَ: «لَا يَزَالُ يُسْتَجَابُ لِلْعَبْدِ مَا لَمْ يَدْعُ بِإِثْمٍ أَوْ قَطِيعَةِ رَحِمٍ مَا لَمْ يَسْتَعْجِلْ، قِيلَ: يَا رَسُولَ اللهِ، مَا الاستعجالُ؟ قَالَ: يَقُولُ: قَدْ دَعَوتُ، وقَدْ دَعَوتُ فَلَمْ أَرَ يَسْتَجِيبُ لِي، فَيَسْتَحْسِرُ عِنْدَ ذَلِكَ، وَيَدَعُ الدُّعَاءَ».

٦٧- قَالَ رَسُولُ اللهِ صَلَّى اللهُ عَلَيْهِ وَسَلَّمَ: «ثَلاثَةٌ لَا تُرَدُّ دَعوتُهُم:

الله عليه وسلم - فقال: يا رسول الله، مَنْ أحَقُّ الناس بحُسْن صَحابتي؟ قال: «أمُّك»، قال: ثم مَنْ؟ قال: «أمُّك»، قال: ثم مَنْ؟ قال: «أمُّك»، قال: ثم مَنْ؟ قال: «أبوك».

٥٩ - قَالَ رَسُولُ اللهِ صَلَّى اللهُ عَلَيْهِ وَسَلَّمَ: «مَنْ كانَ يُؤمِنُ باللهِ واليومِ الآخرِ فليُحْسِنْ إِلى جارِه».

٦٠ - قَالَ رَسُولُ اللهِ صَلَّى اللهُ عَلَيْهِ وَسَلَّمَ: «ما زال جبريل يُوصِيني بالجارِ، حتى ظننتُ أنه سيُوَرِّثُه».

٦١ - قَالَ رَسُولُ اللهِ صَلَّى اللهُ عَلَيْهِ وَسَلَّمَ: «مَن كانَ يُؤمِنُ باللهِ واليومِ الآخرِ فلا يُؤذِ جَارَهُ».

٦٢ - قَالَ رَسُولُ اللهِ صَلَّى اللهُ عَلَيْهِ وَسَلَّمَ: «ما آمَن بي مَن بات شبعانَ وجارُه جائعٌ إلى جَنبِه وهو يعلم به».

٥٦- عن أنس بن مالك، رضي الله عنه، جاء ثلاثةُ رَهْطٍ إلى بُيوت أزواج النبي - صلى الله عليه وسلم -، يسألون عن عبادة النبي - صلى الله عليه وسلم -، فلما أُخْبِروا كأنَّهم تَقالُّوها، قالوا : فأينَ نَحنُ مِن رسولِ الله - صلى الله عليه وسلم -، وقد غُفِرَ له ما تقدَّم من ذنبه وما تأخَّر ؟ قال أحدُهم : أمَّا أنا فأصلِّي اللَّيلَ أبدًا، وقال الآخرُ : وأنا أصومُ الدَّهرَ ولا أُفطِرُ، وقالَ الآخرُ : وأنا أعتَزِلُ النِّساءَ ولا أتزوَّجُ أبدًا، فجاءَ رسولُ الله - صلى الله عليه وسلم - إليهم، فقال: «أنتم الذين قُلتم كذا وكذا ؟ أمَا والله، إنِّي لأخْشاكم لله، وأتقاكم له، ولكني أصومُ وأفطرُ، وأصلِّي وأرْقُدُ، وأتزوَّجُ النِّساءَ، فَمَن رغِبَ عَن سُنَّتي فليس منِّي».

٥٧- قَالَ رَسُولُ اللهِ صَلَّى اللهُ عَلَيْهِ وَسَلَّمَ: «إنَّ خِيارَكم أحاسنُكم أخلاقاً».

٥٨- عن أبي هريرة، رضي الله عنه، قال : جاء رجل إلى النبي- صلى

السَّمَوَاتِ والأرضِ مائةَ رَحمةٍ، كلُّ رحمةٍ طِبَاقُ ما بَينَ السَّماءِ والأرضِ، فَجَعَلَ مِنْهَا في الأرضِ رَحمةً، فبها تَعطِفُ الوالدةُ على وَلَدِها، والوَحْشُ والطيرُ بعضُها على بعض، فإذا كان يومُ القيامَةِ أكمَلَهَا بهذه الرحمة».

٥٣ - قَالَ رَسُولُ اللهِ صَلَّى اللهُ عَلَيْهِ وَسَلَّمَ: «بَيْنَمَا كَلْبٌ يُطِيفُ بِرَكِيَّةٍ قَدْ كَادَ يَقْتُلُهُ الْعَطَشُ إِذْ رَأَتْهُ بَغِيٌّ مِنْ بَغَايَا بَنِي إِسْرَائِيلَ فَنَزَعَتْ مُوقَهَا فَاسْتَقَتْ لَهُ بِهِ فَسَقَتْهُ إِيَّاهُ فَغُفِرَ لَهَا بِهِ».

٥٤ - قَالَ رَسُولُ اللهِ صَلَّى اللهُ عَلَيْهِ وَسَلَّمَ: «مَا مِنْ إِنسانٍ يَقْتُلُ عُصْفُوراً فما فوقها بغيرِ حَقٍّ إلا سَأَلَهُ اللهُ عز وجل عَنها، قيل: يا رسولَ اللهِ، وما حَقُّها؟ قال: يَذْبَحُها فيأكُلُها، ولا يَقْطع رأسها ويَرمي بها».

٥٥ - قَالَ رَسُولُ اللهِ صَلَّى اللهُ عَلَيْهِ وَسَلَّمَ: «ما مَلأَ آدميٌّ وعاءً شَرًّا من بَطْنٍ، بِحَسْبِ ابنِ آدمَ لُقَيْمَاتٌ يُقِمْنَ صُلْبَه، فإن كان لا مَحَالةَ: فَثُلُثٌ لِطَعَامِه، وثُلثٌ لِشرابِه، وثُلثٌ لِنَفَسِه».

٤٧- قَالَ رَسُولُ اللهِ صَلَّى اللهُ عَلَيْهِ وَسَلَّمَ: «طَلَبُ الْعِلْمِ فَرِيضَةٌ عَلَى كُلِّ مُسْلِمٍ».

٤٨- قَالَ رَسُولُ اللهِ صَلَّى اللهُ عَلَيْهِ وَسَلَّمَ: «مَن خَرَجَ في طلب العلم فهو في سبيل الله حتى يَرجع».

٤٩- قَالَ رَسُولُ اللهِ صَلَّى اللهُ عَلَيْهِ وَسَلَّمَ: «التَّاجِرُ الأَمينُ الصَّدُوقُ: مع النَّبيِّين والصِّدِّيقين والشُّهداء».

٥٠- قَالَ رَسُولُ اللهِ صَلَّى اللهُ عَلَيْهِ وَسَلَّمَ: «لما قضى الله الخلقَ كتبَ في كتابه على نفسه، فهو موضوعٌ عنده: إنَّ رحمتي تغلِب غضبي».

٥١- قَالَ رَسُولُ اللهِ صَلَّى اللهُ عَلَيْهِ وَسَلَّمَ: «الرَّاحِمُونَ يرحمهم الرحمن، ارحَمُوا مَن في الأرض، يرحَمْكم من في السماءِ».

٥٢- قَالَ رَسُولُ اللهِ صَلَّى اللهُ عَلَيْهِ وَسَلَّمَ: «إنَّ اللهَ خَلَقَ يومَ خَلَقَ

بِهِ وَرَجُلٌ عَرَفَ الْحَقَّ فَجَارَ فِي الْحُكْمِ فَهُوَ فِي النَّارِ وَرَجُلٌ قَضَى لِلنَّاسِ عَلَى جَهْلٍ فَهُوَ فِي النَّارِ».

٤٣ - قَالَ رَسُولُ اللهِ صَلَّى اللهُ عَلَيْهِ وَسَلَّمَ: «إِنَّ المُقْسِطِينَ عِندَ اللهِ عَلَى مَنَابِرَ مِنْ نُورٍ عَنْ يَمِينِ الرَّحْمَنِ - وَكِلْتَا يَدَيْهِ يَمِينٌ - الَّذِينَ يَعْدِلُونَ فِي حُكْمِهِمْ وَأَهْلِيهِمْ وَمَا وَلُوا».

٤٤ - قَالَ رَسُولُ اللهِ صَلَّى اللهُ عَلَيْهِ وَسَلَّمَ: «إِنَّ اللهَ رَفِيقٌ يُحِبُّ الرِّفْقَ فِي الأَمْرِ كُلِّهِ».

٤٥ - قَالَ رَسُولُ اللهِ صَلَّى اللهُ عَلَيْهِ وَسَلَّمَ: «مَنْ سَرَّهُ أَنْ يَبْسُطَ اللهُ لَهُ فِي رِزْقِهِ، وَأَنْ يُنْسَأَ لَهُ فِي أَثَرِهِ، فَلْيَصِلْ رَحِمَهُ».

٤٦ - قَالَ رَسُولُ اللهِ صَلَّى اللهُ عَلَيْهِ وَسَلَّمَ: «مَنْ سَلَكَ طَرِيقًا يَلْتَمِسُ فِيهِ عِلْمًا سَهَّلَ اللهُ لَهُ بِهِ طَرِيقًا إِلَى الجَنَّةِ».

من كُرَب الدنيا نَفَّسَ الله عنه كُربة من كُرَب يوم القيامة، ومن يَسَّرَ على مُعسِر، يَسَّرَ الله عليه في الدنيا والآخِرَة».

٣٩- قَالَ رَسُولُ اللهِ صَلَّى اللهُ عَلَيْهِ وَسَلَّمَ: «انْصُرْ أَخَاكَ ظالما أو مظلوما، فقال رجل: يا رسولَ الله أنصرُه إذا كان مظلوما، أفرأيتَ إن كان ظالما: كيف أنصرُهُ؟ قال: تحجزُه أو تمنعُه عن الظلم، فإن ذلك نَصرُهُ».

٤٠- قَالَ رَسُولُ اللهِ صَلَّى اللهُ عَلَيْهِ وَسَلَّمَ: «من احْتَكَرَ طعامًا فهو خاطئ».

٤١- قَالَ رَسُولُ اللهِ صَلَّى اللهُ عَلَيْهِ وَسَلَّمَ: «الكَيِّسُ مَنْ دانَ نفسَه، وعَمِلَ لما بعد الموت، والعاجِزُ مَنْ أَتْبَعَ نَفَسَهُ هَوَاهَا وتمنَّى على الله».

٤٢- قَالَ رَسُولُ اللهِ صَلَّى اللهُ عَلَيْهِ وَسَلَّمَ: «الْقُضَاةُ ثَلَاثَةٌ وَاحِدٌ في الْجَنَّةِ وَاثْنَانِ فِي النَّارِ فَأَمَّا الَّذِي فِي الْجَنَّةِ فَرَجُلٌ عَرَفَ الْحَقَّ فَقَضَى

بيَّن ذلك، فَمَنْ هَمَّ بحَسَنة فلم يعملْها كَتَبها الله له عنده حسنة كاملة، فإن هَمَّ بها وعَمِلها، كَتَبَها الله له عنده عَشْرَ حسنات إلى سبعمائة ضِعْف، إلى أضعاف كثيرة، ومَنْ هَمَّ بسيئة فلم يعملْها، كَتَبها الله عنده حسنة، وإن هو هَمَّ بها فَعَمِلها، كَتَبَها الله له سيئة واحدة».

٣٦- قَالَ رَسُولُ اللَّهِ صَلَّى اللَّهُ عَلَيْهِ وَسَلَّمَ: «تُفْتَحُ أبوابُ الجنَّةِ يومَ الاثنين والخميس، فَيُغْفَرُ لكلِّ عبد لا يُشرِكُ بالله شيئا، إلا رجلا كان بينه وبين أخيه شَحْناءُ، فيقول: أنظروا هذين حتى يصطلحا، أنظروا هذين حتى يصطلحا، أنظروا هذين حتى يصطلحا».

٣٧- قَالَ رَسُولُ اللَّهِ صَلَّى اللَّهُ عَلَيْهِ وَسَلَّمَ: «ألا وإنَّ في الجسد مضغةً، إذا صلَحَتْ صلَحَ الجسدُ كلُّه، وإذا فسدت فسدَ الجسدُ كلُّه، ألا وَهِي القلبُ»

٣٨- قَالَ رَسُولُ اللَّهِ صَلَّى اللَّهُ عَلَيْهِ وَسَلَّمَ: «مَن نفَّسَ عن مؤمن كُرْبة

إلا مَنْ أطعمتُهُ، فاستطعموني أُطعِمْكم، يا عبادي، كلُّكم عار إلا مَنْ كَسوتُه، فاستكسُوني أكْسُكُمْ، يا عبادي، إنكم تُخطئون بالليل والنهار، وأنا أغفِرُ الذُّنوبَ جميعا، فاستغفروني أغفِرْ لكم، يا عبادي، إنَّكم لن تبلغوا ضَرِّي فتَضُرُّوني، ولن تبلغوا نَفْعي فتنفعوني، يا عبادي، لو أنَّ أوَّلكم وآخرَكم وإنسَكم وجِنَّكم، كانوا على أتقَى قلب رجل واحد منكم، ما زاد ذلك في مُلكي شيئا، يا عبادي، لو أنَّ أوَّلكم وآخرَكم، وإنسَكم وجِنَّكم، كانوا على أفجر قلب رجل واحد منكم، ما نقص ذلك من ملكي شيئا، يا عبادي، لو أنَّ أوَّلكم وآخرَكم، وإنسَكم وجِنَّكم، قاموا في صعيد واحد، فسألوني، فأعطيتُ كلَّ إنسان مسألتَهُ، مانقص ذلك مما عندي إلا كما يَنْقُص المِخْيَطُ إذا أُدخِلَ البحرَ، ياعبادي، إنما هي أعمالُكم أُحصيها لكم، ثم أوفِّيكم إيَّاها، فمن وَجدَ خيرا فليَحْمَدِ الله، ومن وجد غير ذلك فلا يَلُومَنَّ إلا نَفْسَهُ».

٣٥- ابن عباس أن رسولَ الله -صلى الله عليه وسلم- قال - فيما يروي عن ربِّهِ - : «إنَّ الله تعالى كَتَبَ الحسناتِ والسيئاتِ، ثم

٣١- قَالَ رَسُولُ اللهِ صَلَّى اللهُ عَلَيْهِ وَسَلَّمَ: «إِنَّ الرِّفقَ لا يكونُ في شيءٍ إِلا زَانَهُ، ولا يُنْزَعُ مِن شيءٍ إِلا شَانَهُ».

٣٢- قَالَ رَسُولُ اللهِ صَلَّى اللهُ عَلَيْهِ وَسَلَّمَ: «تَهادُوا تحابّوا، وتصافحُوا يذهبِ الغُلُّ عنكم».

٣٣- قَالَ رَسُولُ اللهِ صَلَّى اللهُ عَلَيْهِ وَسَلَّمَ: «قال اللهُ عز وجل: كَذَّبَنِي ابنُ آدمَ، ولم يكُنْ له ذلك، وشَتَمَني، ولم يكن له ذلك، فأَمَّا تكذيبه إِيايَ، فقوله: لن يُعيدَني كما بَدأني. وليس أَوَّلَ الخلقِ بأهوَنَ عَلَيَّ مِن إعادتِه، وأمَّا شَتْمُهُ إيايَ، فقوله: اتَّخَذَ اللهُ وَلَدا، وأنا الأحدُ الصَّمَدُ الذي لم يَلِدْ ولم يُولَدْ، ولم يكن له كُفُوا أَحَدٌ».

٣٤- عن أبي ذرٍّ أنَّ رسولَ اللهِ صَلَّى اللهُ عَلَيْهِ وَسَلَّمَ قال: - فيما روى عن الله تبارك وتعالى - أنه قال: «يا عبادي إني حَرَّمتُ الظُّلمَ على نفسي، وجعلتُه بينكم محرَّما، فلا تَظَالموا، يا عبادي، كُلُّكم ضالٌّ إلا مَنْ هَدَيتُه، فاستَهدُوني أَهدِكم، يا عبادي، كُلُّكم جائع

لو أتيتني بقُرابِ الأرضِ خطايا، ثم لَقِيتَني لا تُشرِكُ بي شيئاً: لأَتَيْتُكَ بقُرابِها مَغْفِرَة».

٢٩- أبو هريرة - رضي الله عنه - : أنَّ رسولَ الله -صلى الله عليه وسلم- قال : «يَنْزِلُ رَبُّنَا كُلَّ ليلةٍ إلى سماءِ الدنيا، حين يبقَى ثُلثُ الليلِ الآخِرُ، فيقول : من يَدعُوني فأستجيبَ له ؟ مَن يَسأَلُني فأُعطِيَهُ ؟ مَن يَسْتَغْفِرُني فأغْفِرَ لَهُ ؟».

٣٠- عن أبي هريرة - رضي الله عنه - : أن النبيَّ -صلى الله عليه وسلم- قال : «كَانَ رَجُلٌ يُسْرِفُ على نَفْسِهِ، فَلَمَّا حَضَرَهُ الموتُ، قال لبنيه : إِذَا أَنَا مُتُّ فَأَحْرِقُوني، ثم اطحنوني، ثم ذَرُّوني في الرِّيح، فوالله، لئن قَدَرَ عليَّ ربِّي لَيُعذِّبَني عذاباً ما عذَّبَه أحداً، فلما مات فُعِلَ به ذلك، فأمر الله الأرضَ، فقال : اجْمَعي ما فيكِ منه، ففعلتْ، فإذا هو قائمٌ، فقال : ما حَمَلَكَ على ما صَنَعْتَ ؟ قال : خَشْيَتُكَ يا ربِّ، فَغُفِرَ له بذلك».

٢٥- قَالَ رَسُولُ اللَّهِ صَلَّى اللَّهُ عَلَيْهِ وَسَلَّمَ: «حَقُّ الْمُسْلِمِ عَلَى الْمُسْلِمِ خَمْسٌ رَدُّ السَّلَامِ وَعِيَادَةُ الْمَرِيضِ وَاتِّبَاعُ الْجَنَائِزِ وَإِجَابَةُ الدَّعْوَةِ وَتَشْمِيتُ الْعَاطِسِ».

٢٦- قَالَ رَسُولُ اللَّهِ صَلَّى اللَّهُ عَلَيْهِ وَسَلَّمَ: «رَحِمَ اللَّهُ عَبْدًا سَمْحًا إِذَا بَاعَ سَمْحًا إِذَا اشْتَرَى سَمْحًا إِذَا اقْتَضَى».

٢٧- بَالَ أَعْرَابِيٌّ فِي الْمَسْجِدِ فَثَارَ إِلَيْهِ النَّاسُ لِيَقَعُوا بِهِ فَقَالَ لَهُمْ رَسُولُ اللَّهِ صَلَّى اللَّهُ عَلَيْهِ وَسَلَّمَ: «دَعُوهُ وَأَهْرِيقُوا عَلَى بَوْلِهِ ذَنُوبًا مِنْ مَاءٍ أَوْ سَجْلًا مِنْ مَاءٍ فَإِنَّمَا بُعِثْتُمْ مُيَسِّرِينَ وَلَمْ تُبْعَثُوا مُعَسِّرِينَ».

٢٨- عن أنس بن مالك قال: سمعتُ النبيَّ -صلى الله عليه وسلم- يقول: «قال الله: يا ابن آدم، إنَّك ما دَعَوْتَني ورَجَوْتَني: غفرتُ لك على ما كانَ منكَ، ولا أُبالي، يا ابنَ آدم، لو بلغتْ ذُنُوبُك عَنانَ السماءِ، ثم استغْفَرتَني: غَفَرتُ لك، ولا أُبالي، يا ابنَ آدم إنَّكَ

٢٣- عَنْ عَائِشَةَ رَضِيَ اللهُ عَنْهَا أَنَّ قُرَيْشًا أَهَمَّهُمْ شَأْنُ الْمَرْأَةِ الْمَخْزُومِيَّةِ الَّتِي سَرَقَتْ فَقَالُوا وَمَنْ يُكَلِّمُ فِيهَا رَسُولَ اللهِ صَلَّى اللهُ عَلَيْهِ وَسَلَّمَ فَقَالُوا: وَمَنْ يَجْتَرِئُ عَلَيْهِ إِلَّا أُسَامَةُ بْنُ زَيْدٍ حِبُّ رَسُولِ اللهِ صَلَّى اللهُ عَلَيْهِ وَسَلَّمَ فَكَلَّمَهُ أُسَامَةُ فَقَالَ رَسُولُ اللهِ صَلَّى اللهُ عَلَيْهِ وَسَلَّمَ: أَتَشْفَعُ فِي حَدٍّ مِنْ حُدُودِ اللهِ ثُمَّ قَامَ فَاخْتَطَبَ ثُمَّ قَالَ: «إِنَّمَا أَهْلَكَ الَّذِينَ قَبْلَكُمْ أَنَّهُمْ كَانُوا إِذَا سَرَقَ فِيهِمُ الشَّرِيفُ تَرَكُوهُ وَإِذَا سَرَقَ فِيهِمُ الضَّعِيفُ أَقَامُوا عَلَيْهِ الْحَدَّ وَايْمُ اللهِ لَوْ أَنَّ فَاطِمَةَ بِنْتَ مُحَمَّدٍ سَرَقَتْ لَقَطَعْتُ يَدَهَا».

٢٤- كَانَ رَسُولُ اللهِ صَلَّى اللهُ عَلَيْهِ وَآلِهِ وَسَلَّمَ إِذَا بَعَثَ سَرِيَّةً، قَالَ: «اغْزُوا بِاسْمِ اللهِ، وَفِي سَبِيلِ اللهِ، قَاتِلُوا مَنْ كَفَرَ بِاللهِ، لَا تَغُلُّوا وَلَا تَغْدِرُوا، وَلَا تُمَثِّلُوا، وَلَا تَقْتُلُوا وَلِيدًا وَلَا شَيْخًا كَبِيرًا».
وَعَنِ ابْنِ عَبَّاسٍ، عَنْ رَسُولِ اللهِ صَلَّى اللهُ عَلَيْهِ وَسَلَّمَ: «أَنَّهُ كَانَ إِذَا بَعَثَ جُيُوشَهُ، قَالَ: اخْرُجُوا بِسْمِ اللهِ، تُقَاتِلُوا فِي سَبِيلِ اللهِ، مَنْ كَفَرَ بِاللهِ لَا تَعْتَدُوا وَلَا تُمَثِّلُوا وَلَا تَقْتُلُوا الْوِلْدَانَ وَلَا أَصْحَابَ الصَّوَامِعِ».

٢٠- عَنْ أَبِي هُرَيْرَةَ أَنَّ رَسُولَ اللَّهِ صَلَّى اللَّهُ عَلَيْهِ وَسَلَّمَ: «قَالَ بَادِرُوا بِالْأَعْمَالِ سَبْعًا هَلْ تَنْتَظِرُونَ إِلَّا فَقْرًا مُنْسِيًا أَوْ غِنًى مُطْغِيًا أَوْ مَرَضًا مُفْسِدًا أَوْ هَرَمًا مُفَنِّدًا أَوْ مَوْتًا مُجْهِزًا أَوْ الدَّجَّالَ فَشَرُّ غَائِبٍ يُنْتَظَرُ أَوْ السَّاعَةَ فَالسَّاعَةُ أَدْهَى وَأَمَرُّ».

٢١- عَنْ أَبِي مَسْعُودٍ قَالَ: قَالَ رَسُولُ اللَّهِ صَلَّى اللَّهُ عَلَيْهِ وَسَلَّمَ: «حُوسِبَ رَجُلٌ مِمَّنْ كَانَ قَبْلَكُمْ فَلَمْ يُوجَدْ لَهُ مِنَ الْخَيْرِ شَيْءٌ إِلَّا أَنَّهُ كَانَ يُخَالِطُ النَّاسَ وَكَانَ مُوسِرًا فَكَانَ يَأْمُرُ غِلْمَانَهُ أَنْ يَتَجَاوَزُوا عَنِ الْمُعْسِرِ قَالَ: قَالَ اللَّهُ عَزَّ وَجَلَّ نَحْنُ أَحَقُّ بِذَلِكَ مِنْهُ تَجَاوَزُوا عَنْهُ».

٢٢- قَالَ رَسُولُ اللَّهِ صَلَّى اللَّهُ عَلَيْهِ وَسَلَّمَ: «يَا أَيُّهَا النَّاسُ أَلَا إِنَّ رَبَّكُمْ وَاحِدٌ وَإِنَّ أَبَاكُمْ وَاحِدٌ أَلَا لَا فَضْلَ لِعَرَبِيٍّ عَلَى أَعْجَمِيٍّ وَلَا لِعَجَمِيٍّ عَلَى عَرَبِيٍّ وَلَا لِأَحْمَرَ عَلَى أَسْوَدَ وَلَا أَسْوَدَ عَلَى أَحْمَرَ إِلَّا بِالتَّقْوَى».

١٥- عَنِ النَّبِيِّ صَلَّى اللهُ عَلَيْهِ وَسَلَّمَ قَالَ: «مَنْ لَمْ يَرْحَمْ صَغِيرَنَا وَيَعْرِفْ حَقَّ كَبِيرِنَا فَلَيْسَ مِنَّا».

١٦- عَنِ النَّبِيِّ صَلَّى اللهُ عَلَيْهِ وَسَلَّمَ أَنَّهُ قَالَ: «مَنْ كَانَتْ لَهُ ثَلَاثُ بَنَاتٍ فَصَبَرَ عَلَيْهِنَّ، وَأَطْعَمَهُنَّ، وَسَقَاهُنَّ وَكَسَاهُنَّ، كُنَّ لَهُ حِجَابًا مِنَ النَّارِ».

١٧- قَالَ رَسُولُ اللهِ صَلَّى اللهُ عَلَيْهِ وَسَلَّمَ: «إِذَا مَاتَ الْإِنْسَانُ انْقَطَعَ عَمَلُهُ إِلَّا مِنْ ثَلَاثٍ صَدَقَةٌ جَارِيَةٌ وَعِلْمٌ يُنْتَفَعُ بِهِ وَوَلَدٌ صَالِحٌ يَدْعُو لَهُ

١٨- قَالَ رَسُولُ اللهِ صَلَّى اللهُ عَلَيْهِ وَسَلَّمَ: «يَتْبَعُ الْمَيِّتَ ثَلَاثَةٌ فَيَرْجِعُ اثْنَانِ وَيَبْقَى مَعَهُ وَاحِدٌ يَتْبَعُهُ أَهْلُهُ وَمَالُهُ وَعَمَلُهُ فَيَرْجِعُ أَهْلُهُ وَمَالُهُ وَيَبْقَى عَمَلُهُ».

١٩- عَنْ أَبِي الدَّرْدَاءِ قَالَ قَالَ رَسُولُ اللهِ صَلَّى اللهُ عَلَيْهِ وَسَلَّمَ: «إِنَّ اللهَ أَنْزَلَ الدَّاءَ وَالدَّوَاءَ وَجَعَلَ لِكُلِّ دَاءٍ دَوَاءً فَتَدَاوَوْا وَلَا تَدَاوَوْا بِحَرَامٍ».

١٠ - قَالَ رَسُولُ اللهِ صَلَّى اللهُ عَلَيْهِ وَسَلَّمَ: «مَا مِنْ مُسْلِمٍ يَغْرِسُ غَرْسًا أَوْ يَزْرَعُ زَرْعًا فَيَأْكُلُ مِنْهُ طَيْرٌ أَوْ إِنْسَانٌ أَوْ بَهِيمَةٌ إِلَّا كَانَ لَهُ بِهِ صَدَقَةٌ».

١١ - قَالَ رَسُولُ اللهِ صَلَّى اللهُ عَلَيْهِ وَسَلَّمَ: «مَا مِنْ مُسْلِمٍ يَغْرِسُ غَرْسًا إِلَّا كَانَ مَا أُكِلَ مِنْهُ لَهُ صَدَقَةً وَمَا سُرِقَ مِنْهُ لَهُ صَدَقَةٌ».

١٢ - قَالَ رَسُولُ اللهِ صَلَّى اللهُ عَلَيْهِ وَسَلَّمَ: «مَنْ رَأَى مِنْكُمْ مُنْكَرًا فَلْيُغَيِّرْهُ بِيَدِهِ فَإِنْ لَمْ يَسْتَطِعْ فَبِلِسَانِهِ فَإِنْ لَمْ يَسْتَطِعْ فَبِقَلْبِهِ وَذَلِكَ أَضْعَفُ الْإِيمَانِ».

١٣ - قَالَ رَسُولُ اللهِ صَلَّى اللهُ عَلَيْهِ وَسَلَّمَ: «مَنْ أَصْبَحَ مِنْكُمْ آمِنًا فِي سِرْبِهِ مُعَافًى فِي جَسَدِهِ عِنْدَهُ قُوتُ يَوْمِهِ فَكَأَنَّمَا حِيزَتْ لَهُ الدُّنْيَا».

١٤ - قَالَ رَسُولُ اللهِ صَلَّى اللهُ عَلَيْهِ وَسَلَّمَ مَا أَكْرَمَ شَابٌّ شَيْخًا لِسِنِّهِ إِلَّا قَيَّضَ اللهُ لَهُ مَنْ يُكْرِمُهُ عِنْدَ سِنِّهِ».

مَا تَصَدَّقُونَ إِنَّ بِكُلِّ تَسْبِيحَةٍ صَدَقَةٌ وَكُلِّ تَكْبِيرَةٍ صَدَقَةٌ وَكُلِّ تَحْمِيدَةٍ صَدَقَةٌ وَكُلِّ تَهْلِيلَةٍ صَدَقَةٌ وَأَمْرٌ بِالْمَعْرُوفِ صَدَقَةٌ وَنَهْيٌ عَنْ مُنْكَرٍ صَدَقَةٌ وَفِي بُضْعِ أَحَدِكُمْ صَدَقَةٌ قَالُوا يَا رَسُولَ اللهِ أَيَأْتِي أَحَدُنَا شَهْوَتَهُ وَيَكُونُ لَهُ فِيهَا أَجْرٌ قَالَ أَرَأَيْتُمْ لَوْ وَضَعَهَا فِي حَرَامٍ أَكَانَ عَلَيْهِ فِيهَا وِزْرٌ فَكَذَلِكَ إِذَا وَضَعَهَا فِي الْحَلَالِ كَانَ لَهُ أَجْرًا».

٨- قَالَ رَسُولُ اللهِ صَلَّى اللهُ عَلَيْهِ وَسَلَّمَ: «[كُلُّ سُلَامَى مِنَ النَّاسِ عَلَيْهِ صَدَقَةٌ كُلَّ يَوْمٍ تَطْلُعُ الشَّمْسُ] قَالَ تَعْدِلُ بَيْنَ الاثْنَيْنِ صَدَقَةٌ وَتُعِينُ الرَّجُلَ عَلَى دَابَّتِهِ تَحْمِلُهُ عَلَيْهَا أَوْ تَرْفَعُ لَهُ مَتَاعَهُ عَلَيْهَا صَدَقَةٌ وَقَالَ الْكَلِمَةُ الطَّيِّبَةُ صَدَقَةٌ وَقَالَ كُلُّ خُطْوَةٍ يَمْشِيهَا إِلَى الصَّلَاةِ صَدَقَةٌ وَتُمِيطُ الْأَذَى عَنِ الطَّرِيقِ صَدَقَةٌ».

٩- قَالَ رَسُولُ اللهِ صَلَّى اللهُ عَلَيْهِ وَسَلَّمَ: «لَا يَحْقِرَنَّ أَحَدُكُمْ شَيْئًا مِنَ الْمَعْرُوفِ وَإِنْ لَمْ يَجِدْ فَلْيَلْقَ أَخَاهُ بِوَجْهٍ طَلِيقٍ».

Sayings of the Prophet Muhammad

٤- لَعَنَ رَسُولُ اللَّهِ صَلَّى اللَّهُ عَلَيْهِ وَسَلَّمَ الرَّاشِيَ وَالْمُرْتَشِيَ وَالرَّائِشَ يَعْنِي الَّذِي يَمْشِي بَيْنَهُمَا.

٥- قَالَ رَسُولُ اللَّهِ صَلَّى اللَّهُ عَلَيْهِ وَسَلَّمَ: «تَرَى الْمُؤْمِنِينَ فِي تَرَاحُمِهِمْ وَتَوَادِّهِمْ وَتَعَاطُفِهِمْ كَمَثَلِ الْجَسَدِ إِذَا اشْتَكَى عُضْوًا تَدَاعَى لَهُ سَائِرُ جَسَدِهِ بِالسَّهَرِ وَالْحُمَّى».

٦- عَنْ عَبْدِ اللَّهِ بْنِ عَمْرٍو عَنِ النَّبِيِّ صَلَّى اللَّهُ عَلَيْهِ وَسَلَّمَ قَالَ: «أَرْبَعَةٌ مَنْ كُنَّ فِيهِ كَانَ مُنَافِقًا أَوْ كَانَتْ فِيهِ خَصْلَةٌ مِنَ الْأَرْبَعِ كَانَتْ فِيهِ خَصْلَةٌ مِنَ النِّفَاقِ حَتَّى يَدَعَهَا إِذَا حَدَّثَ كَذَبَ وَإِذَا وَعَدَ أَخْلَفَ وَإِذَا عَاهَدَ غَدَرَ وَإِذَا خَاصَمَ فَجَرَ».

٧- عَنْ أَبِي ذَرٍّ أَنَّ نَاسًا مِنْ أَصْحَابِ النَّبِيِّ صَلَّى اللَّهُ عَلَيْهِ وَسَلَّمَ قَالُوا لِلنَّبِيِّ صَلَّى اللَّهُ عَلَيْهِ وَسَلَّمَ: «يَا رَسُولَ اللَّهِ ذَهَبَ أَهْلُ الدُّثُورِ بِالْأُجُورِ يُصَلُّونَ كَمَا نُصَلِّي وَيَصُومُونَ كَمَا نَصُومُ وَيَتَصَدَّقُونَ بِفُضُولِ أَمْوَالِهِمْ قَالَ: أَوَ لَيْسَ قَدْ جَعَلَ اللَّهُ لَكُمْ

الأحاديثُ باللغةِ العَرَبيّة

١- قَالَ رَسُولُ اللهِ صَلَّى اللهُ عَلَيْهِ وَسَلَّمَ: «لَا يُؤْمِنُ أَحَدُكُمْ حَتَّى يُحِبَّ لِأَخِيهِ مَا يُحِبُّ لِنَفْسِهِ».

٢- عَنْ عَبْدِ اللهِ بْنِ مَسْعُودٍ عَنِ النَّبِيِّ صَلَّى اللهُ عَلَيْهِ وَسَلَّمَ قَالَ: «لَا يَدْخُلُ الْجَنَّةَ مَنْ كَانَ فِي قَلْبِهِ مِثْقَالُ ذَرَّةٍ مِنْ كِبْرٍ. قَالَ رَجُلٌ: إِنَّ الرَّجُلَ يُحِبُّ أَنْ يَكُونَ ثَوْبُهُ حَسَنًا وَنَعْلُهُ حَسَنَةً. قَالَ: إِنَّ اللهَ جَمِيلٌ يُحِبُّ الْجَمَالَ، الْكِبْرُ بَطَرُ الْحَقِّ وَغَمْطُ النَّاسِ».

٣- عَنْ الْبَرَاءِ بْنِ عَازِبٍ قَالَ قَالَ رَسُولُ اللهِ صَلَّى اللهُ عَلَيْهِ وَسَلَّمَ: «يَا فُلَانُ إِذَا أَوَيْتَ إِلَى فِرَاشِكَ فَقُلْ اللَّهُمَّ أَسْلَمْتُ نَفْسِي إِلَيْكَ وَوَجَّهْتُ وَجْهِي إِلَيْكَ وَفَوَّضْتُ أَمْرِي إِلَيْكَ وَأَلْجَأْتُ ظَهْرِي إِلَيْكَ رَغْبَةً وَرَهْبَةً إِلَيْكَ لَا مَلْجَأَ وَلَا مَنْجَا مِنْكَ إِلَّا إِلَيْكَ آمَنْتُ بِكِتَابِكَ الَّذِي أَنْزَلْتَ وَبِنَبِيِّكَ الَّذِي أَرْسَلْتَ فَإِنَّكَ إِنْ مُتَّ فِي لَيْلَتِكَ مُتَّ عَلَى الْفِطْرَةِ وَإِنْ أَصْبَحْتَ أَصَبْتَ أَجْرًا».

بِسْمِ اللَّهِ الرَّحْمَٰنِ الرَّحِيمِ

﴿ وَمَا أَرْسَلْنَاكَ إِلَّا رَحْمَةً لِّلْعَالَمِينَ ﴾

Books by Ibn Kathir & Ibn Al-Qayyim

"The sinner does not feel any remorse over his sins,
that is because his heart is already dead"

* Stories of the Prophets   ISBN 9798774942602
* Inner Dimensions of the Salāh   ISBN 9781643544557
* Seerah of Prophet Mūhammah   ISBN 9781094860213
* Stories of the Koran   ISBN 9781095900796
* The Path to Guidance   ISBN 9781643540818
* Purification of the Soul – Vol 1 ISBN 9781643541389
* Al-Fawaid: Wise Sayings   ISBN 9781727812718
* Heaven's Door   ISBN 9781643541396
* The Ideal Muslimah by Ibn Kathir ISBN 9798834334422
* Koran: English Easy to Read   ISBN 9781643540924
* Characteristics of Hypocrites   ISBN 9781643541358
* Diseases of the Hearts and their Cures ISBN 9781643541129
* Tawbah: Turning To Allah   ISBN 979-8517657411
* The Holy Quran in English   ISBN 979851591373
* Timeless Seeds of Advice   ISBN 9798784652522
* The Lofty Virtues of Shaykh al-Islām   ISBN 9798846178922
* Great Women in Islam   ISBN 9781505398304

www.ingramcontent.com/pod-product-compliance
Lightning Source LLC
Chambersburg PA
CBHW071906070526
44583CB00016B/1865